Saint James of Compostela

Text: Julie Perino
Illustrations: Capucine Mazille
Translation: Barbara Davoust

A long time ago, when the Romans ruled Galilee, Jesus claimed that he was the son of God. One day as he was walking along the shore of Lake Tiberias, he noticed fishermen working in their boat. There were two brothers, James and John, along with their father, Zebedee. Jesus called to them, "Come and follow me and I will make of you fishers of men!" James and John decided to accompany him. James, who became one of Jesus's closest disciples, was nicknamed "Son of Thunder" because of his fiery character. He is also called James the Greater so that he will not be mixed up with another James, called the Lesser because he joined the group of twelve apostles later. James witnessed the miracles of Jesus and stayed with him until the evening of his arrest on the Mount of Olives. After his resurrection, Jesus appeared to the apostles one last time, "Go all over the world", he ordered them, "proclaim the Gospel to all creatures, to all nations, make disciples…" James chose to go to Spain.

After a long journey by sea James arrived in Galicia, a region in north-western Spain. He preached the word of Jesus on the roads of the country, which at that time was governed by the Romans. But nobody took the time to listen to him. By the time he reached the gates of the city of *Cæsaraugusta* — today's Zaragoza — James was discouraged. But Mary, Jesus's mother, came to his help. From her home in Jerusalem, she flew through the sky, carried by angels. With her she brought a marble column — *pilar* in Spanish — that her angels set up on the shores of the Ebro River. She stood on top of the pillar and said to the amazed apostle, "James, I give you this pillar, build a church to shelter it and your mission will succeed!" When Mary had left, James set to work and built the church. He was well rewarded: all those who entered and touched the column were converted! This church still exists in Zaragoza, even though its appearance has changed a bit since James's time. It is the Basilica of Our Lady of the Pillar.

Back in Palestine, James evangelised Judea. There he met Philetus, a disciple of the magician Hermogenes, who decided to give up magic and become James's friend. This made Hermogenes very angry! In revenge, the magician sent an army of terrible demons to capture James. But these demons were powerless before the apostle. Indeed, an angel had tied them up with fiery chains. They were afraid of burning themselves and begged James to free them. James accepted, but on condition that they go and capture Hermogenes and bring him back. Imprisoned by his own demons, Hermogenes recognised his defeat. He threw away his books about magic and he too became James's friend.

In about the year 44 AD, the King of Judea was Herod Agrippa I, who did not like Christians. He had James arrested and condemned to die by being beheaded in Jerusalem. But on his way to the torture James performed a miracle: he healed a paralysed man under the amazed eyes of one of his guards, Josias, who was holding the end of the rope James had around his neck. Seeing the paralysed man walking, Josiah became convinced that he should follow James. He decided to die at his side.

After his death, seven of James's disciples gathered up his body during the night in order to find him a burial place. They took him to the port of Jaffa where they found a little boat without a rudder. They placed the apostle's body in it and set sail, letting themselves be guided by the hand of God. The boat floated all the way to Galicia. Reaching the Ría de Arosa, it went up the Sar River. It landed at Iria Flavia, at the very spot where Saint James had arrived on his first journey to Spain.

The disciples laid the body on a large stone that miraculously hollowed itself out, like soft wax, and shaped itself into a sarcophagus to welcome Saint James.

Wishing to find a beautiful place to bury Saint James, the disciples asked for help from Luparia, a rich lady in the area. But she began by refusing to help them. She sent them to the king of the country, who threw them into prison. James's friends managed to escape. The king and his guards ran after them but, hardly had they crossed the bridge that the seven companions had taken, the bridge collapsed under their feet and they drowned in the river. The disciples once again asked Luparia for help. Pretending to accept, she sent them to Mount Ilicinus, where she said they would find oxen that would help them build the tomb. But really the mountain was a shelter for furious bulls and a dragon. Protected by Saint James, the seven disciples managed to triumph over the dragon and to tame the bulls. They hitched them to a wagon and placed the apostle's body in it. When she saw this, Luparia was converted to their faith. She had her palace turned into a church, where Saint James's tomb was placed.

Years and centuries went by. Everyone had forgotten the story of James. However, at the beginning of the 9th century, angels told the hermit Pelagius about the presence of the saint's tomb close to his home. Then local inhabitants noticed a star shining in the night, showing a specific place.

The bishop of Iria Flavia ordered excavations. And under the old marble arches covered in brambles, James's tomb was discovered. King Alfonso II of Asturias had a church built to contain it. The first pilgrims came to pray there and a city sprang up around it. It is called Santiago de Compostela, from the Latin *Campus stellae*, the "Field of the Star".

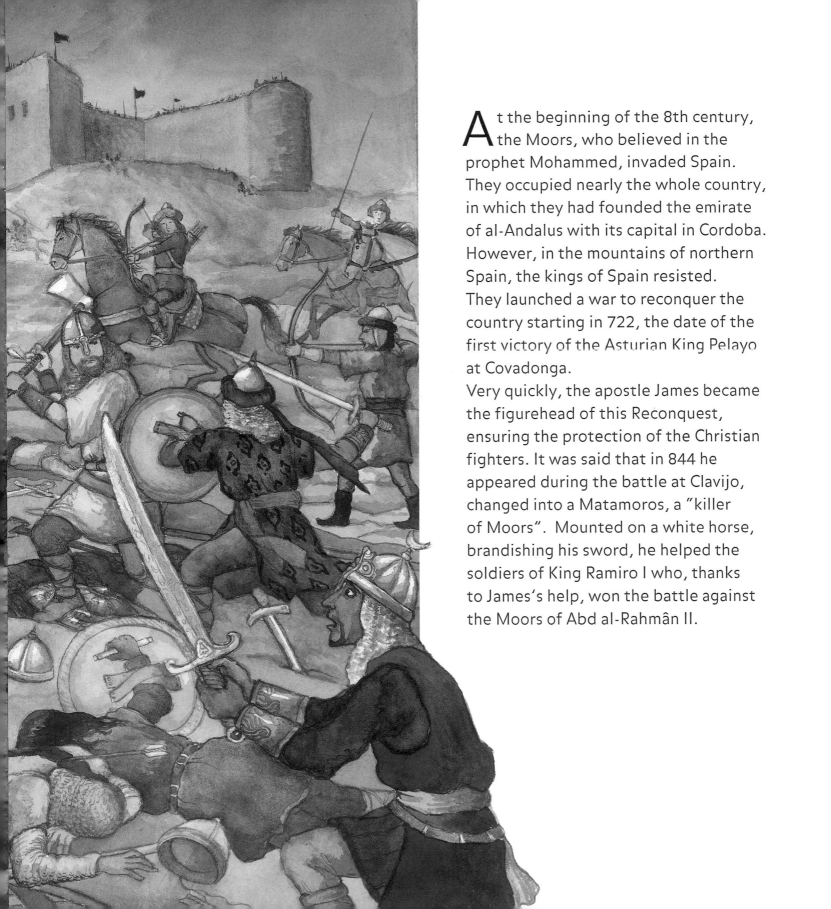

At the beginning of the 8th century, the Moors, who believed in the prophet Mohammed, invaded Spain. They occupied nearly the whole country, in which they had founded the emirate of al-Andalus with its capital in Cordoba. However, in the mountains of northern Spain, the kings of Spain resisted. They launched a war to reconquer the country starting in 722, the date of the first victory of the Asturian King Pelayo at Covadonga.

Very quickly, the apostle James became the figurehead of this Reconquest, ensuring the protection of the Christian fighters. It was said that in 844 he appeared during the battle at Clavijo, changed into a Matamoros, a "killer of Moors". Mounted on a white horse, brandishing his sword, he helped the soldiers of King Ramiro I who, thanks to James's help, won the battle against the Moors of Abd al-Rahmân II.

After the passage of al-Mânsur, there were even more pilgrimages to Compostela. The city's ramparts, houses and the apostle's church were all rebuilt. Starting in 1075 an even bigger church was built by the bishop Diego Peláez. This is the Romanesque cathedral that we can still admire today. Masons, stone-cutters, sculptors and painters worked hard on the site. A brilliant artist, Master Mateo, finished the construction. He provided the building with a porch that has a beautiful, sculpted facade, called the Portico of Glory. At the end of the century, in 1095, the pope accorded Compostela the privilege of being a diocese.

Today's pilgrims are not very different from those of the Middle Ages. Of course, their equipment is better than before. They are no longer afraid of wolves and crossing rivers is much easier because bridges have been built. Today, some do the pilgrimage by bicycle, and sometimes even a little bit by car. Thanks to telephones, their families can get news. But it is still the same need for prayer and peace that guides them. They take the same paths, stopping at the same places as the pilgrims of long ago. Like them, along the way they are happy to find a little chapel with the seashell symbol carved above the doorway. In Compostela, Saint James Cathedral is still beautiful. Before the Portico of Glory, the Baroque Obradoiro facade was added in the 18th century.

And on July 25, the feast of Saint James, a huge incense burner, the *botafumeiro*, swings above the reverential pilgrims, as it did in the 14th century.